STRUGGLE AGAINST

The Story of 500$Fine

by

Gary Llama

OVOLR! / DEBACKLE
RICHMOND, VIRGINIA
USA

ISBN: 978-0-9986977-7-2

Library of Congress Control Number: 2019941954

Copyright 2019

Gary Llama
Richmond, Virginia

Dedicated to the Daly Family. Greg Stephen,
Bo Dillard, George at St Edward's, 500 Punx,
13 Punx, and the South Side Punx

I

He's a warrior. Or at least he thinks he is one, for a seven year old. He stands bare-chested, his young skin milky smooth, and pale. His eyes squinted, looking out, surveying some great vastness. Below each eye, a bagginess from tiredness, though not understood why, factoring in his age. But it has the appearance of Apache war paint. His hand clutches the pump of his shotgun, a 1960s daisy BB gun passed down from his dad. The gun, while menacing, has lost much of the velocity potential, yet still seems dangerous, and deadly, though mainly because of the rusty mechanism of hinges that 'clunk' each time it's cocked. He stands at the edge of his frontier, his yard. And the vastness he is surveying, his col-de-sac, looking for the enemy: IE, any other kid from a better family than his. Better in less violent. Better in less arguing. Better in all ways. En-e-my.

Beside him, his horse, a huffy BMX. Beside that, his other steed: a silver dipped vision skateboard. The top graphic, a fish smoking a cigarette. He grabs the deck and hits down the hill from the cul-de-sac, and at the bottom, tears off into the rough edge of asphalt. The board, balanced on white Gullwing trucks, grinds to a halt, sending him flying off. This is a thing. This is what he does: Board to asphalt edge, grind, fly-off. This is skateboarding.

*

The crowd is a sea of faces, face of people seated on a carpeted stairs of a middle school media room. An auditorium, though too carpeted and to unlike a lunchroom to be daunting. They are awaiting something. A look of anticipation. The stage before them is illuminated by spotlights. On the left corner, a small guitarist, with an even smaller amplifier. He begins. The audience recognizes the tune as 'Don't Cry' by Gun's N Roses. This version however, more out of tune, more slow, and no vocals. It's a painful exercise, as the guitarist makes his way through the song, their collective hope that he pulls it off, carrying him through each part. He finishes, and not too badly, but not amazingly either. The crowd seems satisfied, and gives a warm reception of applause. Good for a 7th grader.

He exits stage left, and begins nervously packing up his equipment. Such an odd thing to do, to be in one moment, the center of an almost mystical ritual, that of the troubadour, playing to the souls of a crowd, and in the next moment, wrapping the rubberized cables of the guitar and amplifier, putting them away like little everyday tools.

'Hey, that was really good', a figure says. The guitarist looks up, and sees a similar sized 7th grader, standing there, hands in pockets, wearing a rock shirt. 'Thanks.' the guitarist says coldly. He can't take compliments. In all honesty, he's surprised the boys who regularly bully him, whom he noticed in the crowd, hadn't just rushed the stage and attacked him. And here, yet again, he was vulnerable. He had been thinking, since weeks before the show, about all the areas of the performance in which he would be vulnerable. A backstage attack seemed likely, being kicked and punched amidst the backdrop of a literal school music performance backdrop curtain. Head hitting the worn wooden floor.

'We should Jam together sometime', the stranger said. 'Yeah, O.. kay..' the guitarist replied slowly, realizing this person was actually being friendly, and not part of an advanced ploy to engage in violence. And with that, the stranger walked away. 'How will I find him?' the guitarist thought to himself, 'He didn't give a number'...

*

     Obviously, it was relatively easy for them to find each other. This was the 7th grade, in a suburb in Virginia, on the south-side of Richmond. They began a friendship, which courted and tested each other. Many questions about favorite bands where asked. And of TV shows, and movies. They eventually began sitting together at lunch, the first day of which, would be a bonding experience beyond anything the little guitarist had known. See, for every day of lunch, there would come a time when an 8th grader would walk by, and on his way to his table, pass by the guitarist. And in passing, he would smack the guitarist on the back of the head. The lunch room had began to anticipate this, and the pass and smack, would bring about a dull in volume, then a small laugh, the back to normal. It had become a normal part of the routine of lunch, like standing in line, or putting up your tray following your meal. The guitarist, feeling very vulnerable, had began to try and counteract this by writing very violent lyrics. Like, ridiculously violent lyrics. Hoping the aura, or fucking something, anything, would be channeled to repel this bully. Because outside of that, there was no end in sight for this. It had been occurring for months, and there were still many months left of school. A physical altercation would surely lead to the guitarist's death, he had assured himself of this fact.

But on the first day that the guitarist and his new friend sat together at lunch, something happened. When the bully passed by to take his daily smack, the bullies hand was met with the stocky forearm of the new friend. The bully stopped walking. Stunned. They stared each other down. But before the guitarist could warn his new friend of how tough this bully was, the bully had... walked off.

Holy fucking shit. The guitarist had played this situation out in his head, standing up to the bully, many times. This conclusion never occurred. Where was the life ending beat down. Where was the entire lunch room pouncing on to join in themselves. The bully had just... given up?

The friend looked over at the guitarist, smiled, and then sat back down. Surely, the bully would return and now smack both of them upside the head. Except he didn't. And the next day, he didn't even approach the table on his way to his seat. It seemed to be... over.

This was Patrick.

My best friend.

II

Making music, and recording it, as a kid in the 90s, went something like this: Use anything. For most of us, what we had was low quality cassette recorders, called 'shoe-box' recorders, designed initially for dictation. And then our walkmans, which played back cassettes well, but had no record function. For some of the craftier of us, we could 'fake' a multitrack recording, by playing back the Walkman while playing a different part, and recording both to the shoe-box recorder. Then put the tape from the recorder into the Walkman, play it back, add another part. This worked, but it resulted in A LOT of hiss on the cassette.

However, My new friend Patrick had something else. A computer.

Now it still wasn't multi track, meaning it only recorded what was happening at the time in stereo, and it only had one input, as stereo one.

However, the lack of hiss opened up a new world for us. And that was empowering. This new world of recording seemed limitless to us. So now, with the technical aspects solved, we began working on the creative aspects.

Patrick had a great sense of humor. And he loved pointing out the absurdity inherent in abuses of positions of power. He drew these cartoon panels, hilarious stuff, of any authority figure we encountered that showed such absurdity. The main targets: Our vice-principal, and our gym teacher. We would spend hours going over the cartoons he had drawn, and they were a hit with his friends in the neighborhood. Accordingly, it seemed like a great place to start for writing music. So we began with songs about the vice-principal, the gym teacher, then expanded.

During that Christmas holiday, we ended up having a marathon of sleepovers at his house. We wrote and recorded, day and night. In the end, we had around 17 songs. It was our 'Christmas' tape, which had very little to do with Christmas, but seemed an appropriate way to redeem ourselves with family on the effort expended. As kids, I guess we needed an occasion to justify the recording. Otherwise, simply making an 'album', would seem delusional. There were no fans telling us they wanted it. There was no record label paying us to make it. And being musicians wasn't our 'job'. Eventually we would learn that you make albums because you want to, not for anything else.

We distributed this 'Christmas' tape to friends and family. We played it for folks at school. We were 13 or 14 years old, and had made our first 'album'. Despite the importance of this not being fully realized by us, we were excited, and we were stoked on future possibilities.

***

Much like the excuses needed to make an album, the occasions for playing music live, for middleschoolers, were relegated to two different times. One, the school talent show. And the more elusive 'Battle of The Bands'. The 'Battle of the Bands', theoretically, has bands play, be judged, and compete to win. The practical aspect is that your band gets to perform. Ideally, winning a Battle of the Bands seems like something one would want to do, but the effect of the award was lost on us. Did any of our favorite heavy metal bands win a Battle of the Bands? No? So why should we care? In effect, the Battle of The Bands phenomena served to further perpetuate the idea that bands our age shouldn't be playing actual concerts. And really, who were we kidding, we couldn't play the local coliseum like Metallica or Megadeth would. Unfortunately, the Battle of the Bands was generally limited to High School bands, so for it, we had to wait. So we set our sights on the OTHER opportunity: The talent show.

This talent show would mark a year since Patrick and I had become friends. After all, it was at this particular event, that we met. For this one though, we would play together. And we would try to play with a full band. Patrick, being the more socially connected of the two of us, managed to find us a drummer, a kid named Matt. He had a kit, and he had been playing a little while. Socially, he was more popular than us, and was very into soccer, which I had played as a kid, but had sucked at. Matt, however, agreed to play only under one condition: That his friend Langdon be allowed to play as well. Not to be outdone, we also had another friend of ours, Duncan, join us to play. Duncan was more advanced musically than us, and had louder equipment. So all together, it probably wouldn't be that bad.

The big difference with a talent show, however, becomes apparent when you watch it. It's a bit of everything. From dancers, to singers, to baton twirlers, to perhaps comedy, it was something of everything. And then the musical acts, which were usually put on as last ditch efforts, kamikaze performances by kids who never knew if they would play again. The resulting performances are generally horrible. Not to be outdone, we turned all our amps as loud as they would go, and played the shit out of instruments, in a battle royale that would not be mistaken for a band performance, but rather, as four or five instrumentalists playing simultaneously. But it was fun.

At the conclusion of the performance, we talked with Matt and Lang about further playing. They seemed up for it. And so we made plans to start a venture: a band. We learned of an upcoming Battle of the Bands, being held at a church, and basically repeated the same lineup, this time minus Duncan, and this time with a singer. The repertoire would be, like the talent show, a group of cover songs. However, upon beginning to play, the singer got scared and left our area of the floor. And with that, I stepped up to the mic, and became a singer. I did not know how to sing, had never really tried to sing, and I was NOT good at it. However, if that was what I needed to do to play my guitar, and play my guitar with this band, then that is what I would do. It was scary. The whole thing was scary. But singing, even scarier. That show I'd learn about performance as combat, and singing in non-staged venus, as the crowd moshed and moved, and mic would come flying into my face. I concluded the show with a bloody mouth and aching teeth. But that feeling, mixed with the adrenaline and physical exhaustion coming from playing your heart out, against fear, to a room of kids, became something I would relish, and embrace.

***

To a kid, the most important thing a band may have is their name. Next to that, their logo. Because for kids, music is as much about the music as it is the codified signalling to others of the meanings and implications of that music. And we were no different. Patrick and I both loved bands that took the art of 'branding', seriously. And none was better at it than Metallica. I mean, they are called 'Metallica'. A Metal band. With their jagged logo. And not to be outdone, Megadeath. Different logo, same idea. However, when you are naming your own band, you tend to forget these principles, and mainly because you just want to play so bad, will go with anything. Hence why most kids have awesome music on their Walkmans, wear shirts with awesome logos, but are playing in bands with horrible, terrible names. It's because they are too excited. And because they don't understand the process or importance of such things. So was with us. When Patrick suggested the name 'Golden Llamas' for our band, we were like "Great. Awesome! Now we have a name". From what I understand, the name came from some friends, as one of them had a llama incense holder or something, and it seemed funny. Little did I know that goddamn name would go on to define my life, to the point of me writing 'Llama' on the birth certificate of my daughter 20 years later. As a kid, these things are lost on you. But with our name, we now had a functioning band.

Our band practices occurred at one of three places: Pat's house. Matt's house. Or Lang's house. And generally, we rotated in order to not exhaust our parent's patience. Pat's mom however, began to enjoy having us around, which was the distinct opposite reaction of the other parents. So as time moved on, the equipment began just staying at Patrick's house. And eventually, earned a permanent space in the front room of their house. This also meant that Patrick's mom would hear our songs.

And would notice our progress. And with this, we had our first supportive fan, who would give us insight, and positive feedback as we developed into a better band. And that probably helped us keep up the momentum, of both practicing and striving to become better, both as musicians, and as a musical unit. And this was important, because soon we would be recording.

The 'Golden Llama's repertoire up to this point, consisted of songs with the critical perspective of absurdity, that was present in Patrick and I's 'Christmas' tape. Except now we had personal songs. Drawing inspiration from the bands we listened to, we began to delve into 'personal' topics, and political ones. The attempts at this by people our ages, now 14-15, was predictably both hilarious and awful, but also, kind of creepy at some points. Particularly, some of my lyrics. It was through my lyrics that I realized 'Hey, you may have depression, and maybe some other mental issues'. Point taken. Patrick's though, were just hilarious, as well as insightful.

Combined with our recording practices, we ended up making a demo tape. And once we had that, we decided to go play it for the managers of our local indie record store.

III

Soundhole was our local independent record store. I had discovered it's old location, initially called 'Jukebox', in an effort to obtain my heavy metal t-shirts in a better method than the stores like Sam Goodie, would allow. I needed more designs. I also wanted patches. The store did not let me down. It was owned by an older gentleman, and he came to recognize both my mom, and I, as repeat customers. On one visit, he even threw in a pair of 'Megadeath' sweatpants, a gift for my birthday. However, he also told us that he would closing down. The shop would be moving, and his son would take it over, under a new name. It seemed highly unlikely that this new place would be like this one. I was sad.

It was this new location, called Soundhole, where I bought Patrick the self-titled 'Rancid' tape. And by me, I mean my mom bought it. She mentioned that Patrick's birthday was coming up, and asked if I wanted to get him a gift. I remembered the band Rancid, as something that had stuck out to us, and seeing as our friendship revolved around music, and music being the only thing worthwhile to either one of us, it seemed appropriate to get it for him. We had discovered Rancid during a sleepover. We were watching 120 minutes, or Headbanger Ball, or whatever MTV was calling that late night slot at the time, and saw a video of some curious new music. The singer wore a stocking cap. The band was covered in tattoos. And the black and white video featured them running around with a baseball bat, and spray paint, fucking shit up. To a bullied kid, this was VERY interesting to me. I'm a musician. They are musicians. And they are tough. Could I be a tough musician? Could I expel anger at society, instead of myself? Initially, I thought it was a Biohazard video as they were the only musicians I had ever seen that looked anything like this band, that had shaved heads, Mohawks, and spikey hair. But the credit said 'Rancid - Hyena'. So I asked my mom to grab that tape for Patrick's birthday, which she did, and then I forgot about it.

Our first trip to Soundhole went like this. We walked in. The store was much smaller than Jukebox. But way busier. It was covered in fliers and posters for bands we knew, and didn't know. The counter, covered in stickers. We approached the clerk with our tape, and asked him to take a listen. We expected him to be surprised that we had one, I mean, who else is recording their own music. When he said 'Sure', and motioned us over to the speakers, we were a little baffled. 'Oh, they've done this before' I thought to myself. What unfolded next was a learning experience.

The clerk and his assistant proceeded to stand in front of the speakers playing our demo, and listen, emotionless. And as I watched them listen to our tape, the magic and excitement that had blinded my ears to our recording, was washing off. Now I was comparing it to the professional recording I heard minutes earlier out of those same speakers. And now I was hearing fuckups. My fuckups. My horrible voice. Off time drums. Bass parts that seemed disconnected from the rest of the song, and a song structure and tempo that was inconsistent, and lacking. 'Oh fuck', I thought to myself. At the conclusion, Greg, the manager, talked briefly to his assistant clerk, and approached us. Greg said that Bo, the assistant clerk, had a multi-track recorder, and he would help us to make a 'proper' demo. Greg said it reminded him of a band called 'The Stooges', and that once we had a proper demo, we could sell it at his store. So we got Bo's contact information, and set a time to make a demo. In further talking with Bo, we learned he had a band. We also learned they played shows, real shows. This was intriguing. And he let us know of some upcoming shows, and bands we may want to talk to, in similar positions to ourselves. One, in particular, called Knuckle hed, made up of kids just about our own ages, but from a farther out part of the south-side. We thanked him.

    We began practicing for our new demo. We knew we had to tighten up a lot more. We were determined to not experience hearing so many fuckups, so embarrassingly, on one of our tapes, again. We spent the next few months honing our skills, both individually, and as a group. It was tough. There were fights. There were impasses. The band almost broke up a few times. In this we learned we also had to develop interpersonal skills, and conflict mediation that was, realistically, beyond what was expected of our pre-pubescent teens. But we manged to do it. And within a few months, were ready to make the demo, of which we recorded, at Bo's suggestion, at Matt's house, as it had a big garage for the drums, and neighboring rooms for the other instruments. The end result blew our minds. So much more professional. So many fewer mistakes. And it sounded like a real band. On another of Bo's recommendations, we found our way out to a tape wholesaler, who sold cassette tapes in short lengths, of 20-30 minutes, and at lower cost and higher quality, than the typical consumer cassettes available at the store. And with our first duplicated cassettes, we created some rough artwork, and photocopied the covers, which we dropped off as finished products, to the 'local' section of Soundhole. Greg wrote us a consignment receipt, and so began the first distribution of our recordings. We were a real, recorded band now. All we needed were some shows.

IV

Bo proved to be a huge source of knowledge and connection for us. Not only could he connect us with other bands, but with gigs. One of the locations that seemed to have a lot going on, was at a church, St Edward's school. Apparently, the youth director there felt that holding things like 'Battle of the Bands' was a good way to keep youth engaged in good activities, and had persuaded the church to open their doors to all local bands, regardless of background or affiliation. The result were some of the funnest shows we would ever play, and exposure to an entire group of young bands, also playing their own original songs. The bands would setup around the room, and then we would walk around and listen to each band, as they performed. The bands were amazing, and all over the place in terms of talent. Local superstars seemed to appear to us. And the bands, like us, had their own tapes, to which we would buy and listen. These tapes quickly became more important to us than the professional music we had generally listened to. And together, we all had our own culture. Even our own clothing, with bands selling t-shirts, and offering both merch and music, for trade, with other bands. And then there was the audience. Local kids, many of whom would never be allowed to go to a show at a music venue in the city, were given reign to come hang out in this church, where they could hear independent music made by folks their age or just a little older or younger. And with this came a fan base, and fans, and letters, and fan zines, and zine culture. And before you knew it, we were part of a scene.

During all of this, we had been also trying to play at some of the clubs downtown, and upon some chance encounter, got a show at a place called 'Twisters'. Patrick and I had began going to clubs downtown a few months earlier, one of the first of which, was seeing that band Rancid, whom we had grown to like, play with a local band called Avail, and a band called Ipecac. That, however, was at a big venue called the Floodzone, who would become notorious for banning local metal legends, GWAR, due to them getting naked on stage. Apparently, this nakedness offended the local ABC inspectors, and would put clubs at risk of loosing their license to serve alcohol. Those shows, however, were off limits to us due to age. We had to play all-ages shows, which were timed to coincide with the city's curfew for kids, which was 11pm. So for our show at Twisters, it was an early show. And it was uneventful. It was disappointing. The folks who came to see us, well, were there for the other bands. So we played to an almost empty room, except for a few hardcore kids who kept coming back in to see if we were done.

However, it was this curfew that steeped our interest. The city eventually started enforcing it militantly, which was most apparent at the conclusion of one Avail show at the local club, The Metro. At around 10:40 pm, the club was swarmed with police cars and police transport vans, the first I had ever seen. They brought about five of those. And at 10:55, started chasing kids around the parking lot as they departed the ending show. It blew my mind, They were arresting kids and it wasn't even 11 yet. At 10:58, an officer tried to arrest me. At that second, I ran over to a familiar face, Bo, who I saw getting into his car. He was over 18. He locked the door, and looked at me from inside the window with a look of 'Sorry?'. I realized that if I jumped in the car with him, he could theoretically be charged with contributing to the delinquency of a minor, for having contributed to me being out past curfew. 10:59. The officer is now staring me down, and over his shoulder I see my ride arrive. "Jesus Christ" I said to myself and ran over the waiting car of my girlfriend's grandad, whom was running a little late picking us up. The cop half smiled at me as I announced my ride being there.

The trick with the curfew law, was not only that you would get arrested, but you would be penalized with a fine, $500, which obviously, your parents would have to pay, and would then be so angered, as to have to recoup that money from your underage ass either through punishment, abuse, or actual money if you had a job. The effect was clubs began ending 15 minutes early for the early shows, and some clubs just said 'fuck it', and stopped letting minors in at all. The resulting effect, for a while, it seemed like the punk shows we had come to love might not be accessible anymore. It went from there being maybe 5-10 shows per month we would be able to go see, to maybe 1. Feeling like we, as younger musicians, and young members of this scene, were unfairly being targeted, and feeling we had a responsibility to address this, I wrote a song about it. And a few weeks later, one of us suggested a name change. As we were playing proper shows, we should have a proper name. So $500 Fine was adopted. Also, it would probably draw less laughs than 'golden llama's. Fun Fact: At that Rancid show, I ended up talking to their new guitarist Lars, and in that conversation mentioned I had a band, and a demo. When asked what we were called, and told 'Golden Llama's, he laughed, but quickly played it off and offered to go listen to the demo tape with me in their van. But guess what I didn't have on me? A demo tape. Two lessons learned: A) Punk rock is made up of folks who will take the time to be cool to you and b) you should probably have a copy of your music with you, generally, always.

As the band had become more serious, It became clear the next step for us, was to eventually record in a proper studio. But that cost $25 per hour. So we set about trying to raise that money with the only thing a band could properly count on, merch.

To our luck, Matt's dad owned a soccer store. His store made many of the uniforms for the local youth soccer leagues. Accordingly, he had quantity deals with the bulk suppliers of uniforms, who also sold blank t-shirts, as well as equipment to make the shirts in the shop. Matt was also taking art classes in school, and had recently learned of screen printing. So he began practicing, and in the course of this designed a logo for the band. Matt was good with a sharpie, and this logo looked cool. And so we began making some shirts, at first using the transfer processes used by the soccer uniforms, and then also, using the screen printing Matt had begun to learn. Our first shirts: On soccer uniforms, unironically. Now with merch, we really felt like a band. And it set us up for the next weird thing, recognition.

V

As a musician making original music, dealing with criticism can be tough. Here you are, pouring your heart and soul, exposing vulnerability, trying to connect with the listener, to make something that means something to you, and maybe resonates with them. And in this process, you push yourself way past your comfort zones. And in the process of that, you make new comfort zones. Then you put that tape, or that music, out into the world, and it gets reviewed, critically. And you read this feedback in zines, in newspapers, and you hear it from fans, or rabid anti-fans. Sometimes the feedback is in public. Sometimes it's in private. At all times you are listening, and if you aren't used to it, it can hurt.

The worst case scenario of this, would theoretically be, having your recording reviewed, live on-air, on a radio station, with the dj playing a few seconds, then stopping the tape, and just blatantly making fun of it. One of our demos got this treatment thanks to the older brother of our guitarist Langdon, and his friend having a radio show at a local university station. I sat at home, knowing it was going to be played, but not knowing it was going to be reviewed, or torn apart. I had my receiver tuned into the station, and my cassette recorder running when they began playing, and basically, assaulting us. It was the most embarrassing thing I had encountered up to that point. But in the process, I learned a few things. I learned that while getting made fun of for petty shit, like making fun of a lyric by rhyming other things with it, or making fun of the subject matter, hurts, I recognized what they were not making fun of. Like our playing. It was good. Or our song structure, that was good too. Or my voice, despite how vulnerable and untrained I was, it held up. And in that, a trial by fire, I learned how to deal with reviews. What to pay attention for, and what to disregard. To recognize a reviewers intent, and to recognize when they have found an actual issue, versus when they are merely fucking with you. It still hurt, and it still hurts a little today, to see your vulnerability taken as a cold fact and reviewed as such. But you begin to get used to it, accept that it's part of the process.

  The most touching encounters though,

would be with fans. When kids your age, or a little older or younger, come up and tell you that they love a certain song. Or that you inspired them to play guitar. Or that a lyric means a certain thing to them. Those were the golden moments, and they made everything else, every struggle in the process, ridiculously worth it.

But sometimes fans had other things to say. I remember being at a friends house early on, and seeing a letter he and his band had gotten from a fan. And I was like 'oh cool, you get fan letters?'. But in reading this letter, I realized the fan was saying how much he liked my friends band (very nice!) and how cool they were as opposed to shitty poseurs like 500$Fine. I was amazed. It was awkward. The way the kid wrote it, he assumed my friend and their band would agree with it. It caused me to pause. Are the fans trying to pit us against each other? Is it devisive? Also, why does my friend have this hanging on his wall? If I were in that position, of someone criticizing my friend, I would have wrote them back and told them to fuck off. No such reply was issued. And accordingly, I began to learn that in this scene, there was division. There was devsiveness. And some folks would put on a nice face, simply to further their own goals, and then drop you once you had helped them to attain them.

But for some reason, my band and I, were not like that. We remembered what it was like just a few years earlier, when folks took us, as kids, seriously. Even folks like Lars. And we vowed to NEVER do any of that shit to any of our friends. Accordingly, we ended up loosing some friends, whom in all actuality, were not friends. And it made the waters a little more murky when accepting offers and trying to be as open as possible with people. But we went like this: Be as open as we can, but if it is discovered that someone is using us, betraying us, or ultimately trying to manipulate or pit us against something, someone, or some objective: Shut it the fuck down, with no mercy. To paraphrase Teddy Roosevelt, In essence, we learned to walk with a big heart, but backed by a big stick.

VI

When making a record at 15, or 16, or any age that is 'young' for that matter, the realization that both the lyrical content, and the musical content are limited by your own experience, can be difficult to reconcile. In this case, reflective opportunities are decreased. The best approach, is to write honestly, so as to document what you are feeling, as that is a reality that will never change. And this was the approach I took in writing the lyrics for my band. Be it a song about feeding the homeless, dealing with a breakup, or the love of my skateboard, each song was an honest document that I wrote 'fully', IE, I didn't hold back. And that made each lyrical work, a complete work, and something that not only would serve as a platform for expressing myself, but also as a document of the time. Had I chosen subjects more popular to write about, or more specific to a trend or topic occurring at the time, each song would have been limited in effectiveness. This was a decision I came to independently, from my own thinking. But over the years, I realized many other musicians had the same thought. I later learned Ian Mackaye had to come to a similar decision when approaching writing for Minor Threat, the flip-side being the trend of bands to write about President Reagan, which both dated the material, but also limited the scope of the applicability of the emotions or thoughts expressed. This approach ended up informing my lifelong songwriting experience, and is something I still do to this day. It also allows a certain insight when I do decide to approach something more specific, an understanding that this song is dedicated to the now, and may not have legs later.

Musically, we have a different issue: ability. First off, as a songwriter that is both singing and playing guitar, my songs would generally have easier parts to play during the parts I'm singing, than when not. That may seem like a cop-out on paper, but listen to any blue guitarist, and you will hear the same approach, drastically. Sung line /guitar line / sung line / guitar line. The other consideration is the overall ability to make music, and come up with chord patterns and structures that are both unique, and appealing, with the degree of uniqueness usually running contrary to appealing. And that would be appealing in the pop sense. Because while this is punk rock, the style we played, was closer to pop music in structure, than say, jazz. It was designed to be fun, and repetitive, easy to sing a long with. Much like pop music. But where pop music wanted catch-iness to make a hit, we wanted catch-iness to sell the message. We wanted folks singing our lyrics happily, lyrics about important things, and repeating a mantra that was entirely positive and revolutionary. And pay attention to that word Mantra. A mantra is a phrase we repeat to ourselves. It's powerful, because our conscious and unconscious brains tend to believe what they hear. So if your mantra is something of a statement of self-hatred, or self-deprecation, as in a lot of indie / 'grunge' music in the 90s, you are repeating a phrase that will lead to some of that reality for you. I realized this as a listener in my early teens, when I was discovering punk rock. I was seeing two different worlds collide: The indie / grunge world where lyrics were about depression, and self-issues. And the punk rock world, where the issues were more outwardly focused towards society, or more positive in influence. It's the difference between a song like 'Rape Me' by Nirvana, and Fugazi's take on rape culture, 'Suggestion'. One is an empowering statement, where the other is a victimizing one. The realization for me was: Why am I listening to all this depressing music, if I'm already depressed? And in that, I realized the appeal of such songs laid heavier with those that had a hard time understanding their emotions, so seeing their own depression could be powerful. But for me, I was well aware. I lived in an abusive household. I didn't need a song to help me realize depression, I was fighting each day to not kill myself from it, and sadly, from very early on. So when I discovered the power of the mantra, and one with positive subjects that punk offered, I jumped onto it whole heart-idly, and started filling my mind with those positive statements of the hope I saw, and who I wanted to be, instead of the ones that confirmed what I already knew, and was. And this extended into my songwriting. At a certain point, I basically vowed to not put negative energy into my creations. Life was already too negative. The songs, for me would be a place, not to disconnect from my reality, but rather to build a bridge from where I am at, to where I want to be. So they would acknowledge depression, but use my hopes as the guiding point, either in the ultimate spirit of the song, or in the specific solutions explored. And this decision, allowed me something else: to be a kid, from a fucked up home, that was depressed, and yet have this very positive body of work, a very positive contribution. It allowed me a place to feel good and turn my struggle into something worthwhile, something useful for others. And that, in turn, empowered me to not only keep living, and not dwell in depression, but also to work on my own emotional issues later in life, as at a certain point, I realized my own happiness and well being would contribute to better art. Perhaps it wasn't' the most self-compassionate reason to be kind to yourself. But it was a reason. And when fighting depression, if the reason isn't self destructive, then it's probably good enough.

***

Talent wise, we had a whole other set of issues. But not from lack of talent. I will be the first to admit, and this isn't coy or self deprecating, but I was the least talented musically, of any of the rest of the band. Patrick, despite starting out as a guitar player, quickly developed into one of the most amazing bass players I had ever witnessed, let alone, played with. And not for just his age, but at any age. By the time he was 16, he was doing bass runs that, 25 years later, are still impossible for me to play, and goddamn infuriating for great bassists to learn.

Watching him develop into that was amazing. And it came from serious practice. While Patrick was always quick with a joke, and really seemed to enjoy putting aside time to just enjoy life, proactively, he somehow also managed to put aside time to seriously practice, in a way that was both time effective and had the most result for invested effort. And from a songwriting perspective, he did the same. He seriously honed the craft of writing songs. He started with contributing both lyrics and parts to mine. And then I would for his. But both of our individual works eventually became much more solid on their own, so when we would add something to the other, it was because it added even more, which resulted in even more amazing songs. The net result being we had some solid fucking songs that stand up 25 years later. And really for two reasons: yes I guess we were talented. But also, because we put in SERIOUS work. We took that shit seriously. Even to the subject matter. At one point we discussed, what would be 'success' to us, and we came up with this: if we inspire one kid, that is success. And from the feedback we received, we would see success, changing one kid enough to make them come up and personally thank us, at least once every couple months. And then when you statistically realize the amount that would typically thank us, versus the amount that actually changed, we realized THOSE weren't the only kids we were effecting, but rather, a statistical mark of the amount we were effecting. It's an important thing to remember. I've been changed by tons of songs, by many artists. And honestly have let zero of them know that, maybe realistically one or two. It's just not something we generally feel is needed, or accepted, to do. But as a songwriter, I can say that it is the best thing ever to hear about how something you put that much effort into, rang true to someone. Because we basically have no idea what is happening out there. And we live in a vacuum of our own thoughts and conclusions on the realities of our work. Which are really the worst realities, because they have very little to do with the actual way people take the songs, and most to do with our intent, which may not really be that clear in the end result.

The other part of the band that was critical, was our Drummer, Matt. To be honest, if you have a good drummer and bassist, you can basically half ass the rest and it will be ok. But goddamn, if your drummer sucks, it's over. Matt did not suck. Even when he sucked, he played with such heart that you didn't notice, and were impressed with his effort.

Then he went to a Nirvana concert, saw Dave Grohl play live, and was changed forever. Where our drummer would formally fill up areas with busywork, a new drummer was born in Matt. The powerful drummer. And he took that to the ength degree. Matt's kit became a collection of broken heads, dented rims. Which snare is his? The one with the Kevlar head. He did this by a) increasing his physical pressure on the kit and b) by using the actual largest sticks he could find, Fieldmaster sticks. They don't even have a size rating, they are just in a class of their own. Field master. Fuck. And he'd break them about every one and a half songs. Luckily he had a job, because he probably cost himself a small fortune just in heads and sticks. But the result was a powerful drum sound for the band, locked with a powerful bass player. And when you combined my love for 'driving' guitar sounds, and powerful lyrics, we really were something impressive. Even 25 years later, after working in studios for years, recording dozens of bands, it's goddamn impressive to me. There was something uniquely special about us.

VII

That specialness wasn't lost on others. For example, it wasn't lost on the band Cloud 13. Made up of a few punk rockers here in Richmond, older than us, cloud 13 was a power pop punk band. Their singer Leer was as charismatic as one could hope, dripping with punk rock swagger. Bassist Bradley, calm, cool collected, and with a bass style that rang unique. And their drummer Kevin, another person who took their craft seriously, and was very good. Together, they had the same elements as we did, strong rhythm section, but they did it better. I'm not sure how the fuck it happened, but this band took us under their wing. They let us hangout, and in that course helped us get shows, gave us advice, and became great friends of ours. It was one of the most important things in the world to happen to us, to have fellow musicians not only approve of your shit, but to help you and empower you. TO be honest, but supportive. Their support, and friendship was a gift that could not be substituted with anything else. For one, us being so young, anyone taking you seriously, was empowering. But to also be giving you specific supportive feedback, that was very empowering. And then to be giving advice, and sharing resources, it was completely invaluable. And with this we began to have a crew. The 13 Punx. The band came with their own roadies, friends of theirs whom would help them out. And they were the the first of the coolest kids I ever saw. The crew really consisted of three people: Jeff, Balon, and Gabe. Jeff was probably the most standout of the group, because he was the quietest. The first time I saw Jeff, I saw a dude, forearms covered in tattoos, wearing a gas mask, with dreads popping out the top. Why a gas mask? Because this room was filled with weed smoke, and Jeff was straight edge. This wasn't' a gag, Jeff was chilling, and simply didn't want their poison in his face. And you had to respect the fuck out of that. Individual enough to assert his own wishes to the point of visual impairment, but also, accepting enough that he would actually stay there. That was rare to me, and stood out. Ballon looked similar to Jeff, tattoos and dreads, but would smoke weed, and was more talkative. Gabe, was completely different though. Gabe was way more wild, while not having the tattoos, he had the look in his eye. A wildcard. But also a supremely awesome friend and person. And together, with some of their other friends, they had a crew, 13 Punx, which Gabe had tattooed on him. In hanging out, I learned the importance of a crew. What is a crew you ask? Well it's basically a closed gang. Closed in that, they aren't looking for new members. So really its just friends, with a name. But also, with a dedicated expectation of loyalty that most people don't have from their friends. You get taken advantage of, your crew is there for you. Girl breaks your heart? They have kind words for you. Guy hits you in the face? They brought bats. Hanging with them, I saw some of the craziest shit I will ever see go down. And it went down with heart, with love, even if from the outside it seemed insane. And I learned that to a lot of people, they didn't understand the crew mentality, and saw many folks make fun of it, as 'wannabe gangster shit'. It's like this: if you don't get it, you don't need it. Much like a suburban kid doesn't need a gun to get through his day. But if you come from abuse, if you come from a broken family, the appeal of having a group of friends who are your family, who literally fill the holes in your heart with the warmth of their support and love, it's intoxicating. And it leads to crazy shit sometimes. Sometimes you find yourself doing some crazy shit with your crew. For us, it was amazing.

And then when we realize, that like cloud 13, we had a number in our name, and were punks too, we decided to bring this phenomenon back to those closest to us, with 500 Punx. And a similar thing happened, we had a crew. And to this day, there is still a bond. It was a point of pride, in a friendship, in a time, that we held onto and cherished. Sometimes just giving something a name and defining it, allows a pride to develop that can empower and encircle people in a positive way. But like I mentioned, it can also lead to an intoxicating power. Realizing you have the backing of a lot of folks skilled in fighting and weaponry, well, some folks take advantage of it, and unleash it to better their own ego. Usually these folks don't last long in a crew, because that exploitation of resources will be noticed. And really, it's a family. So just like if you spend all your family's money, routinely, pattern behaviors will be adjusted for and remedied. But also, it brought up an interesting phenomenon, criminality. Over the years, I've heard many criticisms of the crews I have been a apart of as being 'wannabe' gangsters. And over time, as some of my fellow crew members took less savvy roads, it began to beg the question, what is authentic criminality? Was my friend, who could literally rob drug dealers without a gun, who went to prison for 10 years for cocaine trafficking, was he a real enough criminal? Or was he fake? Was he fake growing up in group homes, because some of his friends lived in the suburbs? Where his friends in the suburbs soft, or fake, because their parents owned houses there? Or was he allowed to be his own self at any point? The state seemed to think he deserved to be acknowledged of his own self and behavior. And when he died from a drug overdose in the worst part of the city I love, was it with privilege? Was it fake? Was he still a wannabe gangster? Was his intermittent Explosive Personality Disorder, his PTSD, his depression, was that somehow privileged?

If you can sense, it makes me angry reflecting on this. And at the root of it is this, there are different types of people involved in punk. Some love the music. Some love the fashion. But to some people, it's a life changing point. If you were an outcast that came up in abuse, well, you had a recipe to be a sociopath, like the earlier folks who became school shooters. To me, they were kids, that like me, had some issues, but they put their time and effort into a BAD solution. Just like I mentioned about the Mantra, the power of how we apply ourselves, and to what, has everything to do with who we are and what we become. So to me, punk was a place that took that animosity towards society, and turned it into a fuel, taught me helpful mantras, then gave me a scene to unleash the work upon. My end result ended up being making albums, making culture. For less fortunate folks, their contribution was hatred animosity or death. And perhaps most importantly, when you realize that there are others in this that are like you, that need that positive support, that becomes another fuel, and an immediacy emerges in the need to help those around us, those that have chosen punk rock as a place to exist, to help these folks become good human beings. Else, we leave it to entropy, and the emotionally disconnected, money and power hungry mantras of society at large. For me, the punk is someone I will always fight for, and that disconnected society: something I will always fight against.

VIII

An album is a declaration. When we began writing the songs that would become our Forward recording, it was part of the second group of songs we had written as 500$Fine, and the fourth set since starting as Golden Llamas. Golden Llamas, the first tape was horrible. HORRIBLE. Because the songs were horrible. By the second tape, we had adopted the writing style that I found worked for me, writing about things that mattered, and it was better. One song in particular, I wrote about my love for my skateboard, and skateboarding. A simple statement. Something I just assume to be understood as a big part of my life, yet maybe not so apparent to the outside world. So it was highlighting things like that, the super obvious, that seemed fresh for first targets. The first set of songs as 500$Fine shifted that super obvious from the personal, to the political. The song 'Ripp Off' was a statement about being young in punk, and it's where the name 500$Fine came from, as it was sung in a line:

'Out past 11, it's 500 dollars for a fine. You stupid pigs are wasting your time'.

It was as much a statement of political stance, as it was a fuck you, which is sung melodically in the last line of the song.

But by the time we got to the fourth and final set of songs, the band had really developed into something else. We were writing with the long term in mind, and it's evident by the staying power of some of the lyrics. The opening line to 'Learning', the first of those nine songs, illustrates this:

> 'Learning to live with less is a need of all to do / Fuck all of their symbols of status, and refine our souls'.

This song also highlights the collaboration occurring between Patrick and I, with me writing and singing the verses, and Patrick writing and singing the chorus.

> 'Loving your brother, loving your sister / will make you happier than any house on the hill / we've got to unify /we've got to unify ourselves befor it's too late'

It's a simple statement, again, an obvious statement. But something so simple, so obvious, stated in this way can be powerful. And when we reflected on what we wanted this band to be about, it was about things like this.

And so it was. I played in a punk band that

sang about love, and had Buddhist philosophy, while I was struggling deeply with demons far removed from that. It was us putting forth the idea of what our future selves could be, of what we strived to be. It was prescriptive. And it's funny, the older I get, the more these lyrics resonate with me, and my life.

  The Buddhist influence came from a few things. One: Patrick. He was one of the calmest people, not so much in how he acted, but in his NATURE. Perhaps, my nature was inquisitive, or anxious. But his was calm, even when spazzing out. It was solid and calm. Philosophically, He was very into Stoicism, which he had learned about in school. And both him and I, as well as some of the folks we were surrounded by, had adopted ritual type things, like incense, like mantras, like the ceremonial smoking of clove cigarettes, of which we would love to do. And long walks that were both meditative and exhausting. One of our favorite places to walk to, was a new age store called 'Alchemist. Located a few miles down the road, it was there we would buy 'Mishma', a blend of herbs smoked by Native Americans. We would also buy incense, and an amazing ginseng chewing gum. We loved 'Alchemist' because of the calming nature of the store. It was in a outdoor mall, a strip mall, but somehow, it had good energy. It was probably the only place where we could reliably encounter such a thing. So our walks would lead us there, where we would meld with the store, adopting it's calm energy, then walk back, chewing our ginseng gum. It was on those walks that we would talk of our thoughts, tell funny stories from school, and share our hopes of the future. It was the perfect activity for Pat and I, as we were both something of hikers, from years in the boy scouts. Both of us, were scouts. Which seems a little odd to think about now, because I just assumed most people were. But they weren't. And perhaps it was something from that, that contributed both to the diligence of our DIY spirit, and to the sheer audacity of us releasing music so young. Scouts was a place that taught me independence. It taught me a lot of skills, and from there I developed knowledge. And it taught discipline. And by drawing on that knowledge, and applying it in a disciplined fashion, I could do almost anything. By the time I was 12, I had rappelled down a 40-foot tower, gone scuba diving, completed swimming qualifications, worked with rebuilding river bank erosion with the Army Corps of Engineers, and served as quartermaster, holding the keys to the equipment of my troop. Upon meeting Patrick, our first summer venture was in co-leading the archery range at scout camp. Yes, scouting definitely informed a big part of our lives.

But our personal lives did as well, both in our experiences at home, as well as with others. Both of us had big hearts, perhaps bigger than others. Both of us cared immensely for others, and felt things like homelessness, poverty, or abuse of power by authority to be horrendous things that we would tackle at any cost. Me, with behavior against it. Patrick, more with his comedic comics. And with 500$Fine, both of us in song. And this extended to our approach to the band, lending our abilities and songs to any benefit show, or benefit comp, that came our way, with a big focus on the problems facing the city we were so memorized by, as well as it's core issues, like homelessness, hunger, and then more applicable to our generation, the curfew law. To us, music was a vehicle for delivering messages to other people. And it extended to when we'd do interviews with zines or newspapers: where we saw the opportunity to spread the word of good and important things.

IX

Reggae has always had an interesting relationship with punk rock. Before reggae, there was ska. And ska, derived from big band music, was one of the first musical genres that could be called 'Crossover' music. I'm not really a music historian, but essentially, in the late 60s, there was a skinhead movement in England, and the music of choice was ska played by Jamaican immigrants. And those skinheads, well they were both black and white folks. And so you had bands like Simaryp, and The Slickers, playing skinhead ska, talking about rude boys, the Jamaican gun-slinging gangster-type that was featured in the seminal movie 'The Harder They Come', with folks like Desmnond Dekker and Jimmy Cliff making appearances on the sound track. Then in the 80s, with punk rock, you had bands like The Specials, Madness, etc, all playing punk-influenced ska.

I discovered Reggae artound the time I was twelve. To me, it had the same energy as the first genre of music I fell in love with, Rap. The group Public Enemy was, to me, the best 'band' ever. Because they were political. Because they seemed to care. And with their use of heavy metal music, from sampling Slayer, to later playing with Anthrax on 'Bring the noise', I didn't really see this music as a different genre than anything else. It seemed more urgent than the political musings of U2, and more specific and relevant than the lyrics of Metallica or Megadeth. Bob Marley had been politicized by the situations surrounding voting in Jamaica, and accordingly had written a lot of anthemic songs. He was a people's singer, a folk hero So his music, full of politics and love, caught my ear and my heart. However, as a white kid from the suburbs, I realized I had no business playing traditional roots reggae.

When we found punk, and saw the amount of crossover between ska and reggae, and the resulting culture that had developed from it, we were given a nice bed to explore making our own 'versions'. And that journey took us to inviting a horn player on some of our songs, and it also found us new friends.

One friend, let's call him Slick: not because that was his name, but as the activities he may or may not have been involved in, I won't use his real name. Plus, he'd like Slick. Slick was an older Jamaican man. He had a piece in a retail store for a bit, and I believe that is where Matt met him. The store sold music. Matt, already being into Ganja, found it to be a shared interest w Slick. Slick also DJ'd, and culturally, he was a modern-day rude boy, or Rudie. No pork pie hat or any of that, but maybe an outfit of full denim and a beeper. ASlick came to appreciate the reggae style we were making, and we came to appreciate Slicks' insight and feedback into those realms. He'd also tip us onto new music, and one of us actually got to go to Kingston with him, for a bit of an adventure. As the friendship progressed, we considered including Slick in the band in a more formal way, perhaps incorporating his skills as DJ. But we never got the chance to do that before the band was over.

And perhaps here it would be important to talk about the idea of cultural appropriation. To me, the last thing I'd want to do is to mimic something I couldn't understand, especially as a white male. Because typically, white folks have taken black culture and made money with it. But for the ska / punk thing, it essentially came from the mixing of Jamaican immigrants in Britain, and the white British punks, and earlier, 'teddy boy's. So with that, there is an understanding that the music was actually a co-collaboration between backgrounds. And to me, that was a beautiful thing. Of course, theres a big difference between that ska, and suburban kids playing roots reggae. So some judgement needs to be exercised. But it was that mix of culture, as with the rock / rap mix of groups like Public Enemy, that gave rise to new music genres, and new sounds, that put people of different backgrounds, in a place to explore creating music with both new sounds, and new context. And really, that is how culture works. Where we see appropriation get labeled, is where it is blankly appropriated, such as white kids wearing Native American head dress. But when it's mixed, well, that is precisely how culture evolves. British food, for instance, has been influenced by the culture of it's immigrants, to the point where Chicken Masala, an Indian dish, is called the official food of Britain. with other influences being the Kabob, curry, and so on.

So when culture mixes sympathetically, we end up with a richer, larger culture. And we've seen the same thing happen with punk rock. Over the years, punk has gone from something of a new fad, to a DIY culture, over to a musical genre that has been assimilated into mainstream culture, both in sound and aesthetic. Similarly, Veganism, which had a strong hold on the ethics of straight edge hardcore in the 1990s, found influence from both the animal rights bands like Conflict, as well as the Krishna influence of US hardcore bands like Youth of Today, Shelter, and 108. Veganism is much more mainstream now. And I have seen it be changed, from something that was a statement of ethics, to more of a diet to lose weight or gain health. While neither of these movements are an ethnic culture, they do provide some basis for me to witness and understand some of the effects of what cultural intertwining, and the eventual absorption of core values surrounding culture, can do when aborbed into mainstream culture. So in the case of punk, it's made things a little harder to figure out. In the 80s and 90s, wearing a punk shirt meant you were probably culturally on the fringe of society, and wearing such a thing usually indicated other behaviors that would be sympathetic to the underground DIY community, such as being more understanding of LGBTQ lifestyles, or political or ethical philosophies such anarchism or veganism. But these days, the shirt may just mean you like the band. And similarly, 10-20 years ago I would assume anyone whom adopted the title of Vegan would be heavily involved in animal rights activism, wheras today, they could just want to lose weight.

One may wonder, does assimilation like this make the surrounding culture more weak? I think yes, to a certain extent. And in that regard, I think we need to be careful with 'appropriating' things from culture. But also, this melting of culture brings some of the tendencies inherent in smaller cultures to larger cultur: So while today's vegan may not care about animal rights as much, the reality is, every vegan results in less animals harmed. And thought it may seem to weaken the ethics of punk rock when someone just sees it as just music instead of culture, in effect, these listeners are widening the reach of bands that are still involved in punk's DIY culture. So, to me, it's not a simple 'bad / good' dichotomy. But it is something to pay attention to.

(Above) Gary Llama and his sister, Susan, early 80s. (Below) Gary on his birthday, with recordings setup, early 90s.

(Above) Gary 1994

"THEY MADE A WASTELAND AND CALLED IT PEACE"
HARDCORE FROM THE TWIN CITIES
FEATURING EX DESTROY VOCALIST
FELIX HAVOC!!!!!!

JAMES RIVER SCRATCH
500 $ FINE

BRING A EXTRA $$$ FOR  RECORDS DISTRO

TUESDAY MARCH 31 EARLY ALL AGES $5   SHOW STARTS @ 7:00 SHARP

BROUGHT TO YOU BY: RVA PUNK NATION
929 W. GRACE ST. RICHMOND, VA 23220 • 804-353-GAME

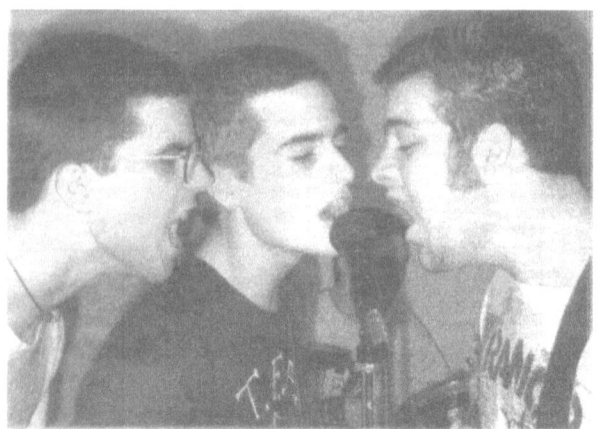

(Above) Andrew Clarke, Gary Llama, and Patrick Daly, at band practice, 1996

(Above) Gary and Duncan Adams, (early Golden Llamas, guitar / vocals for Target For Aggression), late 90s. Photo by Cary Davis

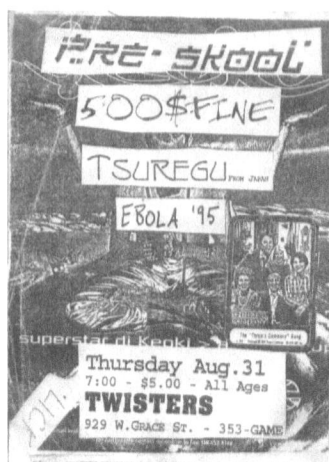

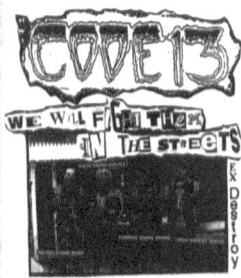

PRE-SKOOL
500$ FINE
TSUREGU FROM JAPAN
EBOLA '95
Thursday Aug. 31
7:00 - $5.00 - All Ages
TWISTERS
929 W. GRACE ST. - 353-GAME

CODE 13
WE WILL FIGHT THEM IN THE STREETS
EX Destroy
Wardance Orange
500 Dollar Fine
Bastard Squad
January 18
6:00 p.m.
5 Dollars
Twisters
929 W GRACE ST
353-GAME

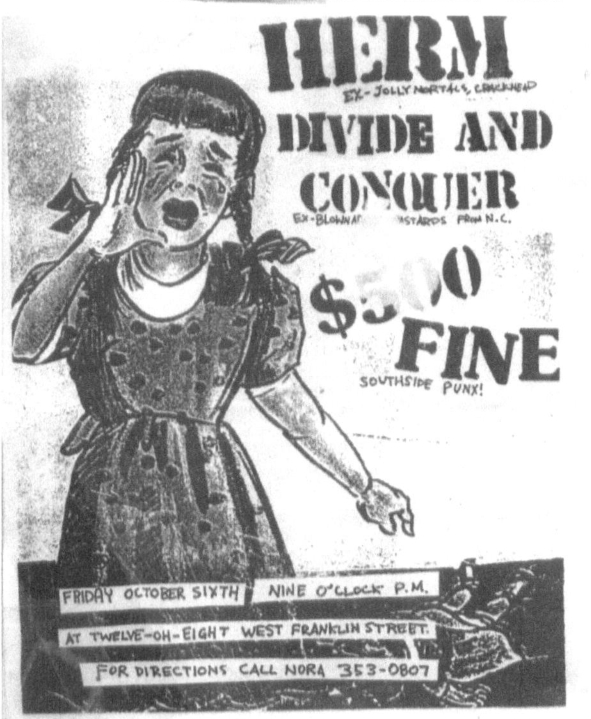
HERM
EX-JOLLY MORTALS, CRACKHEAD
DIVIDE AND CONQUER
FROM N.C.
$500 FINE
SOUTHSIDE PUNX!
FRIDAY OCTOBER SIXTH
NINE O'CLOCK P.M.
AT TWELVE-OH-EIGHT WEST FRANKLIN STREET.
FOR DIRECTIONS CALL NORA 353-0807

line drawing for the RVA Punk Nation

Flier for the benefit show for Patrick Daly, that raised the money for the 500$Fine CD, 'Forward'.

X

In the spring of 1996, a new opportunity had come knocking. The local newspaper contacted us about doing a story on our band and our music. It was to be part of a feature story on local bands, and would highlight 8-10 other bands. To us, this was crazy, as it was for the formal newspaper of our town. The New York Times of Richmond, so to speak. So we took it rather seriously. Before agreeing to do it, we held a band meeting and discussed the interview. We decided that we wanted to make sure the story focused on the politics of our music, and not the novelty of our age. None of us wanted a cutsy story about our age. We didn't want to be patronized for being young. That would set back everything we worked for. Our band, at the core, stood for empowering young people to be taken seriously. People our age had real issues, depression, abuse. People our age committed suicide from these issues. And people our age deserved to have their voice be heard. So the interviews had to focus on issues. Accordingly, we realized we should probably all decided to stick to just a few issues, in order to make sure they were mentioned specifically. So we chose some basic stuff, like our concerns for the homeless of Richmond and the work of Food Not Bombs, as well as our concerns about the way we treat other people in society, be it because of race, gender, sexual orientation, etc. And finally, about our love for the punk rock community as a place to empower people to make and release their own music, without waiting for the major label to do it for us. And to let others know that such things were an option, even to 15 year olds.

And that basis, we told the newspaper we would do the story. They told us they would send over a reporter, and a photographer.

A question we rolled around with a bit: how could we represent the culture we loved, our friends bands, our friends, in the story? If one of us was getting a leg up on mass culture, we wanted to share that with everyone. One easy solution: T-shirts. The photographer would photograph whatever we happened to be wearing, so whatever we wore, would be in the story. 'Cool' i thought. So, knowing my friend Duncan's band was now playing shows, I decided I'd wear a TFA shirt, for his band 'Target

For Aggression'. Unfortunately, TFA didn't have any actual t-shirts. So I made one. I wrote out 'TFA' in letters across a blank blue t-shirt, and drew an illustration below it that seemed to fit. We also learned they would be sending a photographer to a show we were playing at Twisters, so I took care to just dress as I usually would. Unfortunately for me, that included wearing a 'Rastafari' shirt, which I bought because it had an image of Bob Marley on it, and I wanted to share my love of him and his ethics. However, looking back, it was probably more bordering on cultural appropriation than I realized at the time. I just wanted to show my love of Bob and his ethics, but hey, maybe it wasn't the best idea.

When the reporter arrived, it was a bit odd. It's a weird feeling, trying to prioritize and explain EVERYTHING you love and care about to someone with no actual knowledge of you. Luckily we had prepared our issues, but the background stuff, the stuff that was just so apparent to us, well, we realized we had to explain that as well. So it was kind of a frenzy to give a picture of who we were and what we loved. All in all, the interview seemed to go ok, but having been interviewed for zines and such before, I knew you really have no idea what will be written, until you read it. Because no matter what you say, the way it's put together will decide the tone and meaning of the story.

A day or so later, we knew the date the story would run, and began to anticipate its release. A few days later, the story ran.

We woke up that morning, each of us at our different homes, and anxiously ripped apart the paper trying to find it. And there it was. There was a section called 'InSync', which was their 'arts' section, or, 'whats happening section'. Except, it wasn't a story about 10 different bands. It was a cover story on us. With a picture of me on the front, full page, in color, with the words "Proud, Powerful Punk" in big bold letters down the side.

'uh oh', I though to myself.

It's one thing to want the spotlight. It's another thing to get it. We thought this would be a small piece, with around 10 bands featured. We thought the main story would be some shit like 'Richmond has bands, here they are', with little vignettes on each band. What I failed to realize, was that of those 10 bands, we may have been the only ones playing all original music, something VERY typical in punk, but ATYPICAL in young bands of larger culture. So that may have made us stand out. Also, we had already released multiple recordings of original music, wheras most of the other bands may have had a single release. Also, we were regularly playing shows in clubs already, at least one a month, and usually more than that, whereas other bands were not. Also we had ethics, a purpose: Essentially, we had a pretty deep and defined purpose and a lot to say. So they gave us the cover, and the main story. And then they featured a couple little blurbs about other bands. "Jesus', I said, feeling bad for the other bands. But also 'Good Lord', thinking about how I am now being visually represented, a photo from the show of me playing, right there, about 14 inches tall, in color. And with that, I realized that now, a lot of the other punks around town, some who had been playing much longer than us, were now seeing US representing punk rock, in the newspaper. This was a responsibility I hadn't contemplated. What ever we said could either make our scene look ridiculous or awesome. And we thought it was awesome, so I hoped that would come through. And also, being on the cover, folks were gonna be jealous. 'Why not my band' they would think, and I would have to agree, why not their band?. But the opportunity came to us, and we tried to do our best with it, so in that spirit, I read the article.

And it was a good article. There was a little cutesy stuff, but by and large, it focused on our politics, highlighted our age, but not in a patronizing way. It was actually a really good representation. And in the photo above the article, you could see my 'TFA' shirt. 'Awesome! Duncan will be stoked!' I thought to myself.

That morning being a week day, I put down the paper, and got my stuff ready for school, feeling pretty damn good about the entire thing. However, when I arrived at school, I saw many of the kids reading that morning's article. 'WTF?' I thought. 'Like none of these kids read newspapers!'. I realized their parents had probably seen it and given it to them like 'wow there's an article about a band from your school'. Walking through a lunch room, seeing maybe 20 or so kids reading the article, which when they are reading, is showing you a 14 inch tall photo of you on the cover, well it's kind of a psychological nightmare. 'Oh fuck, they are all reading about us' I thought. I sat nervously and waited for class to start.

Over the course of that day I received a lot of feedback. From fellow students, from teachers, I think even at one point the principal called me down to the office to let me know they had seen it. I didn't realize it, but by stating where we went to high school, we were even representing the qualities of our school. Luckily, everyone seemed to think it was good. And then I'd see the older jock kids, pointing towards me, recognizing me from the article. "uh oh", I thought to myself. The last thing I wanted was to be on their radar, I already stood out enough with the way I dressed, but now they for sure knew my name, and my politics. But all in all it was good. Everyone seemed happy with it. When I saw Patrick at school that day, he said pretty much the same thing. We were stoked. When I got home, I called Matt (he went to a different high school) and he echoed a similar sentiment. Then I thought "I wonder what the punk scene will think of it', and realized I wouldn't really know till the next show. In an effort to jump start that realization, I made sure to go to the next show, where some of our friends, and not so friendly folks would be, in order to ease anxiety and get some actual feedback. It was brought up, and despite sensing a little resentment from the less friendly folks, it seemed to be taken in good order. 'Awesome!' I thought, 'Mission Accomplished'.

XI

By the summer of 1996, the 500$Fine had made two new sets of recordings: one, a group of nine songs with engineer Mark Miley, and then a group of four songs made at Charlton studios to help a budding engineer pass his internship. Both sets consisted of the best work we had done to date. But the nine-song grouping was phenomenal for us. Accordingly, we planned to release those songs as a tape in the following months. We didn't want to make another tape, we would have preferred a CD, or better yet, a 12". Hell we would have loved to do a 7". But with the gigs we were playing and the merch we were selling, spending a few hundred for tapes was about all the band's cash box could afford. Especially after emptying it to make the recordings in the first place.

But we were stoked on those nine songs, and began sharing tapes of it with friends. And we started getting feedback. Even folks that had hated us, were now giving positive feedback when they heard the tape. The fact that the article in Insync had come out, and then this tape being circulated, meant that folks that may have not have paid much attention to our band, or known our seriousness, were now taking us as a more serious, defined thing, a band with a purpose, and a band trying to make a difference. Overal, the response was great, and with regards to the music, it seemed we had hit a point where we had finally settled into our own sound.

Over that summer we played a bunch of shows around town, including a blowout show on the last day of school, at Twisters. It was $1 to get in, featured eight bands, and was very hot in that earyl June air. But it was the most amazing show I had ever played. A completely packed crowd. We gave it everything we had. The biggest show we had played previous to that was when we played the Floodzone, a big venue in downtown known for banning GWAR, and according to the venue's sound engineer, when we played there, we were the youngest band to have ever graced their stage. That was cool. But most of our shows revolved around Richmond clubs, with the occasional gig in the south-side at St Edwards, or at someone's house. One time we even went to Charlottesville to play with some punk bands, and had our show interrupted by a Nazi, who the locals informed us was also Jewish. Very odd, but as I've learned, not uncommon to have such conflicts occur in such individuals.

Our hopes for the future hinged on touring, but as we were all in school, we figured it would have to wait until the following summer. So we spent that summer playing gigs locally. When Fall rolled around, we realized our activities would wind down, as we settle back into the groove of the Fall high school semester, and colder Fall weather. But nothing could prepare us for what would happen next.

XII

'Patrick Daly is dead'.

November 16, 1996. My mom is standing over me in my bed. It's 7am. It's a Saturday. I can't believe the words she has just said...

'What?' I asked. "Gary, Patrick died in a car accident last night' she said.

I felt a confusion come over me. Then anxiety. Then back to confusion. Then anger. Then more confusion....

'Are you sure?' I asked.

Of course she was sure. No parent is going to come tell you your best friend is dead without being absolutely sure.

'Yes, Matt's mom just called me'... she said.

But it was worse.

'There were other kids in the car, and they are in critical condition in the hospital' she said. 'Other kids?' I thought. 'Who else?', 'like more of my friends could be dying?' I thought. And with that, we made plans to go to the hospital. I had to see them.

When we got there, the kids were all lined up in a row, except one. "He's in surgery' they said. Before me were some of Patrick's closest friends from his neighborhood. By the time we had arrived, most of the kids had been cleared from the ICU and were now in stable condition. I looked at them and tried to imagine what this must be like for them, having lost their friend, right next to them last night. I was told a story about how a motorist had stopped, and sat with Patrick, whom was more visibly worse off than the others, and how that motorist held Patrick's hand as he died. Apparently when the car crashed, the side of the car he was sitting on had struck a tree, and his head had hit the side window, causing the injury that would end his life.

It was difficult to take in.

The previous day had been Friday, and that day I had been feeling like I was gonna try to hang out, go do something cool that night. I had hit up Patrick to see what he was gonna do, see if he wanted to hang out. He told me that he had plans, him and some friends, going on one of their adventures that evening, and somewhat reluctantly, invited me to come along. I think he knew I wouldn't want to. I was much into adventures. I passed, and decided I would go hang out with this girl I was interested in, but who, on a breakup from a long-time boyfriend, seemed to be working through whether or not she liked me, and whether or not to hold out for a possibility with the boyfriend, again. And so I spent that night slightly cuddling with this cute girl. Then went home. Then woke up to this.

Fuck.

It's hard to process death. Previous to this, the only death I had experienced was the loss of my grandmother. But processing a death like that, seems abstract. I didn't see my grandmother every day at school. I didn't take long walks with her, talking out my dreams and future plans. I didn't discover music with her. I didn't overcome bullying with her. I didn't discover punk rock with her. And I didn't play in a band with her. When Patrick died, I lost a friend, my best friend. I also lost my band. And I lost the only future I could imagine, playing punk rock. In one moment, I realized everything that I was happy about, currently planning for, and long term hopeful for, was gone. Just saying that makes me feel selfish, as it ignores the obvious pain to his family and friends, and it completely ignores what was lost for Patrick himself, which was everything.

In the weeks following his death, my friends and I cocooned. We clung together like we would huddle around a fire, trying to catch a bit of warmth from each other. I didn't understand or question why we did this at the time, I just knew we needed the support. Later I realized it was because the loss of Patrick had left each of us cold and dead inside, our big hearts now wounded, and the love we felt, leaking out of us, the way a hyperthermic body loses heat. And much the same way as a body in crisis, we shook ourselves to try and rejuvenate. We had outbursts of tears, of anger, of rage, at having someone so young, so special, and so pure, taken from us. The crew became a family. 500 Punx became a code to us. My friends now shared a bond, a bond in sadness, in loss, that others couldn't understand. And with that, we became protective of each other the way a mother would care for a wounded baby. Old arguments ceased. Old patterns of behavior stopped. We were at once supportive of each other, and receptive to the support needed to nurture each other threw it. After school each day, We gathered on a friend's porches and sat, sometimes without saying a word. Yet somehow sharing a narrative of sadness and compassion. It was both the saddest time, as well as the most supportive time I have ever experienced. It really showed the effect that his life had on all of us.

As time drew on, the funeral was announced. And following that, life began to slowly turn back to normal. And when it did, I resented it. 'How dare this world go on without him!' I'd think, knowing how irrational the expectation was, but simultaneously knowing that something was owed, in honor, to the loss this world suffered with his passing. Our cocoons broke into smaller groups. For me, it was my friend Jon. Jon had been a good friend for many years, and was in my mind, a brother. And over the loss of Patrick, we became closer than ever. We both effectively dropped out of school, and began spending every waking minute with each other. And we spent our nights together too. We'd just hang, smoke cigarettes, and think. And then we'd do stuff to cheer each other up. And for me, there was no one funnier than Jon. His sense of humor and ability to lambast the absurd was only dwarfed by the size of his heart. As it happened, when Patrick passed, I had no significant other, so this left me ripe for emotional vulnerability, especially when looking back now, and understanding my propensities for codependency and a general lack of self love. And so, as time moved on, I felt the temptations to get into destructive behaviors to numb the pain, like graffiti, drinking, fucking, and fighting. And Jon, with what seemed like an endless river of strength and support, helped to re-center me. I have to say, if it wasn't for his friendship, I may not have made it to where I am today.

XIII

The last thing you want to do when your best friend dies, is move on. That last thing you want to do when your bassist dies, is play another show. But something became apparent: the band had taken on a new meaning to others. It was the vessel into which Patrick had poured his heart and soul. His waking moments resulted in songs, in practice, in booking shows, and everything else required to keep a band operating. Accordingly, if his physical heart had stopped beating, this could be his figurative heart beat. We could carry on the message to some, with the songs. However, we could never think of replacing him. He was a co-founder, co-writer, in short, he was required personnel. Accordingly, Matt and I both knew that this band was over. However, we could play the songs we already had, and we could use those songs to setup some kind of ending, and in the process have a few last moments with audiences to share the message we had all put so much of ourselves into. We felt like there was just a little more to do until we would be ok with laying it down. So we got Jon, and our friend Dan to fill in on bass. Jon played with TFA, so he was family. And Dan played with Indypendant, another band whom we shared a familial bond with. Both of these folks were respectful of the role they were being asked to fill, and knew they were not there to replace Patrick, but rather, to help us share his message. And so we booked a couple of our last shows.

The big question when someone dies is 'what was their legacy?'. You try to figure this out, then honor it. When a musician or artist dies, it's more obvious: Their work. Accordingly, we began trying to figure a way to honour Patrick's work. The first thought, a vinyl record. But to us, it seemed too casual. However, at the time Compact Disc seemed like a more archival type of format. It's coldness seemed to set something in stone. A cataloging of something pressed into the new fangled digital realm. The ultimate tribute. So we looked into what making a CD would require. At the time, the CD as a format was still under active patent, so there were rules about how it had to look, and there was a higher cost to produce one. Hell, even just getting a master cut onto CD-r cost more, with the discs ranging around $30 per disc. Patents are interesting like that. After talking with some friends that had made thier own recordings available on CD, we found a pressing plant, got a price, and then began the work of figuring out how we would raise the money for it.

Somewhere in this process, we remembered our friend George, at St Edwards School. It was a church / school, that for years had held punk shows. Odd right? Well, it went like this. George was the youth director. And one of his jobs was to try and engage the youth. Well, if you were a parent in the 90s, or a school administrator, your biggest fear was drugs and/or crime, as well as idleness, which itself could lead to the former two. So really anything that could get kids together, in a healthy environment, and maybe empower them along the way, well, that would be a great thing. So George decided to bring out the 'Battle of the Bands' event format, and hold some of those at the church. But instead of limiting it to the small cache of musicians at the school, he invited ALL area bands to attend and compete. And in this, he basically held some of the first punk shows many of us ever went to. We didn't give a fuck about winning the competition, we just wanted to play. At some point, this became evident to George, and he started allowing us to book actuall shows there. And it was relatively easy.: so long as enough money was generated to pay the cop that was required for security, we were good. Besides, the church wasn't using the building for anything else those nights, so any money generated was a plus.

The result was fantastic. It was in the suburbs, so many kids were allowed to go, and the fact it was at a church helped tremendously. No worries from the club about underage drinking. No lost alcohol sales from having an all ages show. These were concerns music venues and clubs had. Alcohol was where they made money. George, on the other hand, not having to fund the venue's rent, could actually make money from the admission fee at the door. And instead of alcohol, he opened up the kitchen with soft drinks and water. As a result, many kids got to experience their first live shows here. And as the bands were punk, experience punk rock for the first time as well. And from that experience, many kids started playing music, knowing that they too could play here someday. It was like a little ecosystem.

So when we contemplated raising money for the CD, we knew a St Edwards show would be the only way to do it. We talked with George, and he said that the school would be willing to donate all of the profits they would make that night, directly to us. And with that, we set about booking the bands and the show.

Booking such an event could be a horribly anxiety-ridden endeavor. I had to routinely NOT think about the significance of the event, and instead, just break it into little jobs to complete: Call this band back, ask this band, confirm that band etc. And just selecting the bands was stressfull: do I ask friends, do I ask all the local bands? What do I do? Well, once I mentioned it to some bands, and they mentioned it to their friends, I started getting requests from bands that wanted to play. In the end, I think it was around 12 bands. Going farther into it, I also wanted it to have a double meaning. Not only a gathering for Patrick, but a gathering for something he believed in. So I announced it as an 'Anti-Nazi Gathering'. This was something that was occurring at the time, by punks in an effort to effectively do 'show of force', a signal of anti-racist sentiment to any would-be white power punks or skins that would possibly take notice. Gatherings of solidarity against racism, essentially. And before Patrick's death, doing things like this, and Anti-Racist Action, a more formalized group framework for such 'shows of force', were things we had been discussing with the band. Because, with a counterculture like punk being on the fringes, there have been issues with nazis over the years, with racist fringe groups, either infiltrating scenes, or attacking them. Making shows into pro-active stances like this, let the racists know that we were mindful of their bullshit, and not willing to stand by and let it occur.

  And continuing that focus: IE, what can we help with while honouring Patrick, we began to consider the profits made from the CD, and that it would be cool to donate them to a cause we believed in. And for that, We decided RVA Punk Nation would be the best recipient. The RVA Punk Nation was a collectively-run organization, that had been assembeled a year or so earlier, in an effort to open an all-ages club in the city, for punk bands to play at: For the punks, run by punks. The group came together around the time the City was closing down many of the local clubs due to alcohol violations., which also coincided with the City's crackdown on curfew. As most of the folks involved in punk understood the importance of punk as a positive force in the lives of youth, and the role that all-ages shows play towards that, the group was formed with a bit of urgency. There were other punk venues which served as models of what the Punk Nation was trying to do, with 924 Gilman Street and ABC No RIO being the more successful of these endeavors. So, as I was already involved in the Punk Nation, I suggested to the the Nation the idea of offering our CD's proceeds as a benefit to them. Of course, they were flattered by our offer and accepted it. From there, we just needed to put together the album's artwork, have the show, and then send all the files plus music to the pressing plant. But the big question remained: Would we raise enough money?

    We found that out in one night, in a few hours, in short order. We had raised (and this in 1997 dollars) over $3,000 dollars that evening. We couldn't believe it. However, one of the things St Edwards liked to do, was write down the names of the folks coming in, and write the amount they paid. And in looking over that sheet, we noticed some interesting donations. Such as individuals paying $15, $20, up to even $100 to get into a show that cost $5. And some people, Like George himself, donating, If I remember correctly, around $1,000 dollars. We were humbled. Looking back, I should have maybe expected that, but it never crossed my mind. After all, this WAS a benefit show in Patrick's name, so for many, this was their chance to give something to someone they lost, and in the process, help solidify a big part of his life.

Like I said, it was humbling.

XIV

Nearly a year would pass between that benefit show and the release of the actual CD. Part of it was that making covers back then, was hard. None of us had a computer or the required skills to put together a CD cover, disc image, and assemble them in the formats that the pressing plant required. Luckily, we found a friend, Barrett, who in the course of running his own metal label, had developed the skills, tools, and experience to make the process happen. And he offered it for free. Unfortunately, all these great skills meant he was quite busy, and that meant we had to work around his very busy schedule. Following that, we would have to get the CD mastered, but before that final step, we had another idea.

Before Patrick had died, we had been working on a few new songs. Two in particular, and they were great. We had attempted to record one earlier in tthe year at Charlton, but didn't have lyrics, so it was left unfinished. But there was also a new song that Patrick had written that had become the joy of our later practices. It was called 'Compassion'. I didn't know what the lyrics were, but had heard bits through our PA and the PA at shows, and knew they were really good. This was Patrick's own song. One he had written himself lyrically, as well as most of the music to. I had contributed the verse guitar part. So after his passing, I asked his mom if we could have a look at the lyrics, which he had kept in his lyric folder. But instead of letting me look, she gave it to me. 'You can have this' she said. What I found in there, well, was all of the lyrics to the songs he had been working on. Among the binder was rough ideas, almost finished works, and really detailed, most likely finished, works. But outside of the chords notated, I had no idea what any of them were to be played like. And so I sat there, looking at what was essentially the songs that we would have been introduced to in the future months of our band, had he not passed. It was a weird reality to contemplate. So much that I had to stop myself from thinking about it. The one question I do not allow of myself is 'What if?'. I avoid this because I know it relies on speculation, and speculation, no matter how informed by pervious experience, is devoid of the magical serendipity so present in life.

Like speculation probably could have told me that we would hold Patrick's funeral at a church, but it wouldn't have told me about the meteor shower that also coincided, or the fact that when I would talk to him in my head, a star would should across the sky upon looking up, everytime, almost creepily, to the point that when I explained this phenomenon to my friend, and just all of a sudden pointed towards the sky, we both saw a star cross our horizon, sending chills down both our spines. Speculation also doesn't account for idiosyncrasies, like when I asked Thomas from the punk band Inquisition to attend the funeral, whom Patrick and I had looked up to growing up, it didn't account for him sharing with me some meaningul thoughts on Patricks passing, while sitting outside the funeral itself (Thomas had an aversion to churches). And speculation could not have foresaw the importance rain would hold on my life, from that rainy night forward, that would become a thing I would find solace in. Even my future ex-wife would say 'Good things happen, when it rains'.

So with that green, three-ring binder of Patrick's songs, all written in Patrick's handwriting, I found the lyrics to 'Compassion'. And Matt and I booked time with the engineer we had used on our two previous recordings, Mark Miley, , and went in to record 'Compassion'. In setting up the recording time, we also learned that Patrick's love interest, an amazing young girl named Deanna, well, her father, a singer-songwriter, and her, had come up with a song about Patrick, called 'Butterflies'. Accordingly, we agreed to record this, as anything that was from the heart, needed to be on the CD, genre be damned. And then in the last hours before we were set to record, I found myself writing a new song. A much different song than I had ever written, played on a borrowed acoustic guitar, about my experience growing up with abuse. Did it have anything to do with Patrick death? Not directly. But it was the product of his friendship, his love, and the loss of him that cemented in me both the courage to address it, and to put it out into the world. The arrangement also set the direction for my own solo records, which I would begin working on in the following years.

  And with that, we did the session, had the songs mastered, and sent them out to the pressing plant for production. During production, I had also learned that due to copyright infringement concerns, every CD must have a record label assigned to it, in order to hold responsibility. When I explained we didn't have a label, they told me to make one up. And so I came up with the name, 'One Voice, One Life, Resist!'. Lengthy, but an exact description of the ethics and morals I felt embodied the spirit of what we were doing. And in that moment, I created the record label I would run for decades, and still run to this day.

When we knew the ship date of the CDs, we began planning the final show, at which we would finally release them for sale. The show itself would be a benefit for the RVA punk Nation directly, and the CD profits donated as well.

I remember going to that show. I had just gotten off of work, from delivering pizzas. I had my mohawk hidden under my work hat, and I stood at the back of the room, watching the first bands of the night play, and remembering the first time we played there: The anticipation we felt. The awe we had towards other bands, each doing their own thing. And the hopes we had for ourselves. Here I was, 17 now, watching a new group of young kids, ages 13 and 14, see punk rock occur for the first time. It brought a huge smile across my face, and I knew Patrick would have been proud.

XV

In the years since his passing, I've tried to contemplate what his life meant to me. This book is the culmination of that process for me. Patrick really was the most kind, and big hearted person I had ever met. He was calm and stoic, yet energetic and hilarious. He was emotionally balanced, abnormally so, both for his age and in general. Likewise, he was enormously talented as a musician and bass player, both for his age and in general. As I would later work in studios, I'd notice how exceptional our band had been. It was something that was easy to see individually, such as Pat's bass playing. When I recorded more drummers in the studio, I began to understand how rare Matt's talent for the drums were as well. I had the chance to record him when he was working with a later band, and it blew my mind both how good he sounded, and how powerfully he played. Perhaps, I would recognize something outstanding about my own lyrics or guitar playing, but I'm hindered in the respect that self-evaluation is almost impossible, and even then, is further hindered by my own self-esteem issues and issues with loving and appreciating myself. And it's on those notes, notes that Patrick used to to echo to me, that I really feel the loss of him.

He was my best friend. And he was my music partner, which is a weird way to describe someone you worked alongside of to share and enliven the world around you, through music. He was just SO important to SO much of my life.

But I carry on. And I mean, I carry him on. I keep a little bit of his spirit, his ethic, in everything I do. When i write a song, I aim for the heights he helped me aim for. When I deal with a difficult situation, I try to imagine his advice on the subject and undertand it. And when I work with bands, either in studio or with the label, I would think back to the music we shared together, and remind myself of both the sacredness, and importance of what making music holds to artists both musically and as human beings. In short, he keeps me humble. And where I may second guess myself, or question the validity of something I am doing, I can generally call upon the memory of him to gain some insight into ways to approach almost anything.

Since Patrick's passing, I have also lost other

friends and family, and this process, of carrying on their memory becomes a way in which I can help their spirit continue to influence the lives of others. Whether it be adopting a certain trait, such as smiling at people more, or donating to certain funds that they would have cared about, or perhaps it is in giving folks a chance, that normally I would not, simple out of my own fear. These little actions, adopted from our past friends, help us to learn lessons, and in the course of life, make the world a little bit better place.

I'm going to be very honest here and admit that I don't know how to end this book. Anything I write doesn't seem to be enough, because to an extent, it seems to be a tribute to my friend. And it can never be enough. So knowing that, I'm just going to end it with the best I can do, right now, and that is this:

In the course of your life, you are going to meet some interesting people. And some of those people will touch you a way that expands your life in an amazing way. Be thankful for them. Because at some point, we will lose them. It's how life works. Someone once said, it is the loss of the beauty of a persons life, that causes us to cry at death. But experience is never lost. We must cherish our lives as much in the current day, as we do for our past. And have faith that our future, will be one in which many possibilities wait. And for that to be most fruitul, we must always remain open to noticing, and valuing those new and serendipitous experiences.

TL:DR Don't get jaded.

With love....
Gary Llama

www.ingramcontent.com/pod-product-compliance
Lightning Source LLC
Chambersburg PA
CBHW020429010526
44118CB00010B/486